RUNNING THE RACE

A Three Act Play On The Life Of Paul The Apostle

R A J   H A N S

WESTBOW
P R E S S®
A DIVISION OF THOMAS NELSON
& ZONDERVAN

WestBow Press books may be ordered through booksellers or by contacting:

WestBow Press
A Division of Thomas Nelson & Zondervan
1663 Liberty Drive
Bloomington, IN 47403
www.westbowpress.com
844-714-3454

Cover Illustration by Stephanie Dowling
@art.by.steph.d
stephanie.dowling@ucdconnect.ie

ISBN: 979-8-3850-1985-4 (sc)
ISBN: 979-8-3850-1986-1 (e)

Library of Congress Control Number: 2024903809

Print information available on the last page.

WestBow Press rev. date: 03/11/2024

For:
Nathan, Emma, Sophie and Liam whom my wife Jane and
I pray will run the race with conviction and stern resolve

AUTHORS NOTE

There is no fee if you would like to perform this play. There are no rights required. All I ask is that you kindly let me know that you will be performing it. I'd love to see it.

CAST OF CHARACTERS

Paul the Apostle: A man aged from 30 - 50.

Timothy: A man in his 30s.

Luke: A man in his 40s.

Stephen: A man in his 30s.

Josiah: A man in his 50s.

Wife of Josiah: A woman in her late 40s.

Child 1 & 2:   Josiah's children aged 10 and 12.

Ananias: A man in his 50s.

Cripple in Lystra: A paralyzed man in his 40s.

Barnabas: A man in his 40s.

Priest of Zeus: A man in his 60s.

Lydia: A woman in her 40s.

Sarah: A woman in her 30s.

Rebecca: A woman in her 30s.

<u>Salome</u>:	A woman in her 20s; A soothsayer.
<u>Felonius</u>:	A man in his 50s; Salome's employer.
<u>Barak</u>:	A man in his 50s.
<u>Magistrate</u>:	A man in his 50s; A judge.
<u>Aide 1, 2</u>:	Two men; The Magistrate's aides.
<u>Rufus the Jailor</u>:	A man in his 40s; A jailkeeper.
<u>Agabus</u>:	A man in his 60s; A prophet.
<u>Philip</u>:	A man in his 50s.
<u>Ruth</u>:	A woman age 24; Philip's daughter.
<u>Mary</u>:	A woman age 20; Philip's daughter.
<u>Elizabeth</u>:	A woman age 16; Philip's daughter.
<u>Rachel</u>:	A woman age 18; Philip's daughter.
<u>Tertullus</u>:	A man in his 40s; A lawyer.
<u>Felix</u>:	A man in his 50s; Roman ruler.
<u>Festus</u>:	A man in his 50s; Roman ruler.
<u>Agrippa</u>:	A man in his 60s; A king.
<u>Berenice</u>:	A woman in her 50s; Agrippa's sister.
<u>Esther</u>:	A woman in her 70s; Wife of Onesiphorus.
<u>Priscilla</u>:	A woman in her 40s.
<u>Aquila</u>:	A man in his 40s; Priscilla's husband.

<u>Voice of Jesus</u>:	A voice of a man in his 40s.
<u>Man of Macedonia</u>:	A voice of a man in his 40s.
<u>Jewish Man 1 & 2</u>:	Two men in their 40s.
<u>Crowd Members 1-8</u>:	Eight men in their 40s.
<u>Visitors 1-3</u>:	Three men in their 40s.
<u>Guard 1-6</u>:	Six men in their 40s.
<u>Elders 1 & 2</u>:	Two men in their 50s.
<u>Woman Servant</u>:	A woman in her 30s.

<u>Scene</u>

Various locations in the Bible Lands.

<u>Time</u>

29 AD - 64 AD.

ACT 1
Scene 1

SETTING: The Temple area in Jerusalem.

AT RISE: STEPHEN is kneeling and is surrounded by Sanhedrin Council members in a Judean courtroom setting. PAUL is standing to one side. Others are also watching the proceedings. STEPHEN's arms are outstretched as he is making his defense before the Council.

NARRATOR

In the early days of the Christian church, the twelve apostles chose seven men to serve the daily needs of the church. These were men filled with spirit and wisdom. One of these men was named Stephen, a man full of faith who did great wonders and miracles among the people. Certain members of the synagogue hired men to bring false accusations against Stephen and as a result he was put on trial before the Sanhedrin.

STEPHEN

(In the middle of his speech)

… as you all know God appeared unto Abraham and showed him the land that his people would inherit. But he also said that his descendants would be slaves for 400 years. Isaac and Jacob came after Abraham and knew about the same promise. Jacob had 12 sons who sold their brother Joseph into Egypt.

CROWD MEMBER 1

(Many in the crowd generally murmuring agreement to what STEPHEN has said so far)

Yes that's true. Thanks be to God for Joseph. He saved our people, so he did!

STEPHEN

Then there was a famine and Jacob and his family ended up in Egypt where Joseph was second in command to Pharaoh. When they were in Egypt, the time of the promise that God had made to Abraham was coming closer.

CROWD MEMBER 1

(Crowd murmuring in agreement)

Yes and so it was.

STEPHEN

By this time Joseph was dead and our people were throwing their sons in the river! That's when Moses was born.

CROWD MEMBER 2

(All nodding and agreeing with STEPHEN at the mention of Moses)

Yes, yes, yes … Moses … praise God.

STEPHEN

Pharaoh's daughter saved him and brought him up as her own. When he was 40, he thought the people would know that God had sent him to rescue them. But they didn't! He had to run away for 40 years. Then God appeared to him in a burning bush and told him to return to Egypt to rescue his people. Moses obeyed and brought them out of Egypt through the Red Sea. He suffered with them for 40 more years in the wilderness. During that time, he received God's commandments and gave them to the people.

CROWD MEMBER 1

Moses was a great man. Praise be to God! Moses! Moses!

STEPHEN

He also told them that someday … someday, God was going to raise up a prophet that would really deliver them …

(STEPHEN pauses and looks upwards with reverence)

And yet the people said they wanted to go back to Egypt! So Aaron made a calf and said that the calf was God! So the people started to worship this calf!

CROWD MEMBER 2

(Crowd starts to get restless)

Steady on now young man ... that's not quite true ... myths and the like, you know ...

STEPHEN

In fact for years and years the people worshiped all sorts of gods! So God told them that they were going to get carried away into Babylon.

CROWD MEMBER 2

Hey, why bring that up? What does this have to do with your defense?

STEPHEN

Moses had built a tabernacle for God and King Solomon had built him a house and yet God doesn't live in a tent or a house! Heaven is his throne and the earth his footstool - what sort of house could ever hold him?

CROWD MEMBER 1

(Crowd getting louder)

Wait a minute now, I know you! I've heard you say blasphemous things about the temple before. I heard him with my own ears!

STEPHEN

You always resist God. You do the same thing that your fathers did!

CROWD MEMBER 2

I know him too, I heard him say that Moses was a liar. That's an insult to God!

(Crowd getting more restless and agitated)

How dare you say these things?!

STEPHEN

Name one prophet you didn't persecute!

CROWD MEMBER 1

Hey stop this now! You've gone too far!

STEPHEN

Your fathers killed the prophets that told us about the coming of the Messiah ... and now, you have betrayed and killed the Messiah himself!

CROWD MEMBER 2

(Shouting loudly to drown him out)

Away with him! He's not fit to live!

STEPHEN

(Looking up towards the sky)

Yes I see him. I see the heavens opening and my Lord Jesus standing at God's right hand. Praise be to God!

CROWD MEMBER 1

(Many in the crowd cover their ears so that they cannot hear him. They rush over to STEPHEN and drag him out of the court. Lots of screaming and shouting ensues)

Grab him! Shut him up!

(BLACKOUT)

(END OF SCENE)

ACT 1
Scene 2

SETTING: Outside the city.

AT RISE: The crowd drag STEPHEN to an open area. His hands are tied. They leave him standing in the middle and then step away from him to one side. PAUL is standing at the edge of the crowd.

CROWD MEMBER 1

(A few men in the crowd throw their coats at PAUL's feet as they pass by and start collecting stones from the ground)

Take back what you said! Moses was not a liar! We didn't kill anyone. That's just nonsense! What gives you the right to try and condemn us?

STEPHEN

(Looking upwards, saying nothing)

CROWD MEMBER 1

Repent of your lies you vagabond! Repent now or there will be consequences! OK, you had your chance!

CROWD MEMBER 2

Let's show him what we do to blasphemers! This is what Moses would have done. Yes, yes … praise God for Moses and the Law! Do it in the name of Moses!

CROWD MEMBER 1

(They all look in PAUL's direction for permission)

Well Paul? What says the council?

PAUL

(Looks at them and nods in approval)

CROWD MEMBER 1

Let justice be done! The time for repentance is over!

CROWD MEMBER 2

(Starts throwing stones at STEPHEN. As they hit him time and time again, STEPHEN is hurt and starts to stagger. He is bleeding)

You blasphemer!

CROWD MEMBER 1

See if you can hit him in the face and shut him up once and for all!

PAUL

(With a mocking look)

No one can defy God's justice. No Pharisee would ever have shed the blood of the prophets like you say. And how dare you lecture us on what Moses said – we know the Law better than anyone!

CROWD MEMBER 2

(Stones continue to be thrown and STEPHEN is hurt more and more)

Well said Paul! Praise to the Law! Praise to Moses!

STEPHEN

(Groaning and bleeding badly - barely able to stand. He speaks as loudly as possible)

Lord Jesus! Receive my spirit!

CROWD MEMBER 1

Get him again! He's almost down! Praise to Moses! Praise to the Law!

STEPHEN

(Falls to his knees)

Lord, do not hold this sin against them!

(Dies with one final groan)

CROWD MEMBER 2

(Stones still being thrown)

I think he's had it. One more to make sure! Murderers of the prophets, are we? Call Moses a liar will you? Take that to your God you blasphemer!

CROWD MEMBER 1

Is he done? Is he dead?

CROWD MEMBER 2

Whatever he is, it serves him right for defying Moses.

CROWD MEMBER 1

(A few start to leave and grab their coats from PAUL'S feet)

Thanks for taking care of my coat - wouldn't want to get blood on it!

(Grins and laughs loudly. Others join in speaking to PAUL)

CROWD MEMBER 1

Yes, well done young man! You've done God a great service today. Praise to the Lord, Praise to Moses.

PAUL

Praise to Moses and the Law!

CROWD MEMBER 2

(Crowd all shuffles out, jeering as they go. One man mockingly throws another stone at the body of STEPHEN)

Back to the market now. The work won't get done by itself.

CROWD MEMBER 1

The sleep of a laboring man is sweet!

CROWD MEMBER 2

Huh!

(Laughs at that statement)

PAUL

(The crowd is gone. PAUL stands and looks at the body of STEPHEN)

Death to all those who defy Moses and the Law!

(Spits in the direction of STEPHEN'S body and walks away)

(BLACKOUT)

(END OF SCENE)

ACT 1

Scene 3

SETTING: A room in a house during Biblical times.

AT RISE: A group of people are gathered in a house. There are two children in the group as well. There is a door to the outside at the back of the room. JOSIAH is teaching the group.

JOSIAH

And there are many, many more prophecies in the Law, the Psalms and the Prophets regarding the coming of Jesus Christ, the Messiah. Let's see how well everyone has been listening. Does anyone recall who prophesied that the Messiah would be a king?

CHILD 1

I think it was Balaam?

JOSIAH

Yes, you are correct .. even though he was hired to curse Israel, he spoke a prophecy of the coming king. Alright, where do we learn that he would be from the tribe of Judah?

CHILD 2

From Jacob's prophecy over his son Judah!

JOSIAH

Well done .. do you remember what it said?

CHILD 2

Yes father, "The scepter shall not depart from Judah, nor a lawgiver from between his feet, until Shiloh come .."

JOSIAH

Ah yes, until Shiloh come … very good … OK, who told us where he would be born?

CHILD 1

The prophet Jonah!

JOSIAH

Jonah?

CHILD 2

No silly, it was Micah!

CHILD 1

(Dejected)

Oh yes right …

JOSIAH

And what did he say?

CHILD 1

That the coming Messiah would be born in Bethlehem.

JOSIAH

Well ... you were listening indeed. Did all these prophecies come true according to what was said?

CHILD 1, CHILD 2	OTHERS
Yes, yes!	Yes! Yes of course!

JOSIAH

And ... so where was Jesus born?

CHILD 1

Bethlehem, of course!

JOSIAH

Yes, yes! And there are so many more we have not discussed ... OK, one last prophecy about Jesus ...

PAUL

(Bursts into the room with two guards)

Everyone stay where you are and don't move – we're armed!

(The others about to get up sit back down and stay seated. JOSIAH remains standing)

You!

(PAUL motioning to JOSIAH)

You are obviously in charge here. Did I hear you talking about the one they call Jesus?

JOSIAH

Yes we were speaking of some of the prophecies regarding his coming. I'm sure that you know …

PAUL

(Raises his arm and cuts him off abruptly)

Enough! You've been warned that no one is allowed to speak about that deceiver, have you not?

JOSIAH

Well .. uh ..

PAUL

Do you dare to defy the synagogue? False teachings are an abomination to Moses and the Law. Why are you teaching about this Jesus when you've been told not to?

JOSIAH

I was just sharing with my family and friends about how Jesus is my Lord …

PAUL

(PAUL cuts him off again)

Jesus is not Lord, the One True God is Lord - there is no other! By your arrogance do you contradict the creator of heaven and earth?? Does your blasphemy go so far?!

JOSIAH

Well I do not consider it to be blasphemy...

PAUL

What YOU think matters little! The Sanhedrin upholds the law - and you have broken it! And you teach others also to defy the council - that makes you the ring leader of this Nazarene sect.

(Points a finger in his face)

Do you deny it?

JOSIAH

It was not my intention to defy anyone - only to speak of the Messiah ...

PAUL

He was not the Messiah ... but a deceiver! Did he restore the kingdom to Israel?

(Pauses)

Well, did he or not?

JOSIAH

No but that was never the point of the promised seed ..

GUARD 1

(Cuts him off)

Are you going to lecture him on the Scriptures? Do you know who
this is? This is Paul, a Pharisee of the Pharisees! Of the tribe of
Benjamin! No one knows the Law better than him! Are you better
than the great Gamaliel who taught Paul?

PAUL

(Grabs JOSIAH's arm)

In the name of the God of Israel, I ask you now, Will you deny this
deceiver Jesus?

JOSIAH

In all good conscience, I cannot deny my Lord ...

PAUL

(Throws JOSIAH to the floor, the two guards hold him down)

I command you to say that he was a fraud!

GUARDS

(Pushing him flat on the floor)

Deny him now! Deny him!

CHILD 1

No father! What are they doing? No!

CHILD 2

Mother?!!

WIFE OF JOSIAH

He has done nothing wrong ... please, not in front of the children ...

PAUL

(Pushes JOSIAH'S wife aside)

Step aside woman! This man has defied the living God and will pay for his mistake. Did you think you could do this and we wouldn't find out about it? Don't you know that I serve the True God and he sees all? You can't hide from him.

(Turning back to JOSIAH)

Now, one more time - will you deny this charlatan? I ask you before God, will you deny him?

GUARD 2

Say it now and you will go free. Say it! Deny him!

JOSIAH

God, I ask you, in the name of Jesus Christ - please help us now ...

PAUL

Enough of this!

(Puts his foot on the back of JOSIAH'S neck while he is on the floor and presses down)

JOSIAH

(Moans in pain)

PAUL

Last chance! Will you deny Jesus? Will you recant? Do it now!!

JOSIAH

But ...

PAUL

OK guards, up with him.

GUARDS

(Guards grab him by the arms)

OK, on your feet you knave! Get up!

PAUL

Take him to the cells!

WIFE OF JOSIAH

No, please, you cannot! He's done nothing wrong.

PAUL

Is that right? Take her as well!

(Grabs her by the arm and pushes her to the door)

CHILD 1   CHILD 2

Father!   Mother!

(The others hold the children. The guards drag JOSIAH and his wife out the door)

PAUL

(Looks back before exiting)

You cannot defy God with your blasphemy! Take heed the rest of you. Go and cry to your Jesus!

(BLACKOUT)

(END OF SCENE)

ACT 1
Scene 4

SETTING: On the road to Damascus.

AT RISE: PAUL with three others talking as they walk
                along the road. Two of the men are the same
                guards that were with him at the house of
                JOSIAH.

GUARD 1

Oh, how much further is it? This business for the High Priest can
get tedious and tiring at times.

GUARD 2

(Pointing off into the distance)

Not far now - Damascus is just over that hill and off in the distance.
I can almost smell the gardens.

GUARD 1

Excellent - I can't wait to get some of that Roman wine.

GUARD 2

Wonderful idea - I might even bring some back for my wife … along with some of those juicy apricots for the children.

GUARD 1

Why are the apricots of Damascus better than the apricots of Jerusalem?

GUARD 2

Because they are closer to my mouth!

(All the men laugh)

GUARD 1

Stop! Stop - you're making me hungry.

GUARD 3

You're always hungry …

GUARD 1

Well, it is midday already and we haven't eaten since we left Jerusalem.

PAUL

All in good time, all in good time men. Let's not forget why we're here, alright?

GUARD 3

Do you have the letters Paul?

PAUL

Yes of course - signed by the High Priest himself. I'll tell you, he has no love for these vagabonds terrorizing our good people. He said himself, "Bind all those that you find and throw them in the dungeons at Jerusalem". That'll put an end to their offenses!

GUARD 1

Yes, yes! True enough!

GUARD 2

Perfect - well done Paul. You sure have his ear. Say, what ever happened to that man we took to the cells just after last Sabbath?

PAUL

(Looking up makes a gesture with his hand across his neck to indicate that he had been killed)

GUARD 2

Hmmm … I'm not surprised, he was a fairly obstinate fellow, wasn't he? And his wife?

PAUL

She was released with a final warning … not my decision.

(There is an alarming sound and a bright light appears around PAUL)

GUARD 1

Oooohh ..

GUARD2   GUARD3

Ooohhh…   Whaaaat ..

(The guards all crouch down unable to speak anymore)

PAUL

(Falls to the earth and looks upwards towards the light, trembling in fear)

JESUS

(A voice from above)

Paul! Paul! Why are you persecuting me?

PAUL

Who, … uh, Who are you Lord?

JESUS

I am Jesus whom you are persecuting.

PAUL

(Trembling and astonished with his eyes closed shut)

JESUS

Rise up now, up on your feet.

PAUL

(Gets up, his head still bowed down and his eyes closed. The GUARDS also stand up and look bewildered at the voice which they do not understand)

JESUS

I have appeared to you to make you a minister and a witness of what you have seen and what you will see. I will deliver you from the people and send you to the Gentiles. I want you to open their eyes so that they may turn from the power of Satan to God and receive forgiveness of their sins and an inheritance in heaven by believing in me. This is your purpose. Now go to Damascus and it will be told you what else you are to do.

(The bright light disappears)

GUARD 1

What was that! Did you see that light?

GUARD 2

Yes, yes – but what was it? Whose voice was that? And did you hear what he said?

GUARD 3

No I did not. It was a strange voice - I could not understand what it said.

GUARD 1

I did not either. Paul?

PAUL

(PAUL slowly and deliberately opens his eyes)

That light, that light was so bright ... I, ... I cannot see. I am blinded. I am blind! Help me!

GUARD1   GUARD2

(Run over and take PAUL by the arms)

GUARD 3

Are you sure Paul?

PAUL

Yes, yes ... please help me.

GUARD 3

OK men, let's get to Damascus as quick as we can! Paul needs help. Careful where he walks.

(BLACKOUT)

(END OF SCENE)

ACT 1
Scene 5

SETTING: Two rooms in two separate houses in Damascus.

AT RISE: In one house PAUL is sitting in a chair. A woman is standing beside his chair holding a tray with food and water. In the other house, ANANIAS is praying on his knees.

WOMAN SERVANT

Sir, it has almost been three days and you have not eaten and have had nothing to drink … please, it is for your health.

PAUL

(Shakes his head and holds his head in his hands. The woman walks out looking over her shoulder at him, shaking her head)

Lord, Lord, what has happened to me? What am I to do? What am I to do? Hear me Lord.

(Kneels next to the chair and starts to pray quietly)

JESUS

(Voice speaking in the house of ANANIAS)

Ananias? Ananias?

ANANIAS

I ... I am here Lord.

JESUS

Rise up and make your way to the Street called Straight, to the house of Judas. You will find a man there called Paul of Tarsus and you will find him praying.

(PAUL looks in the direction of the house of ANANIAS as if he can see what is going on)

During his prayers he too has seen a vision - a vision of a man named Ananias ... coming to him and laying his hands on him so that he may see again.

ANANIAS

Oh Lord! I know about this man and what I've heard is not good. They say that he has done many evil things to your people in Jerusalem. Do you know about that Lord?

(Realizes who he is speaking to and mumbles)

Well, yes ... well er ... I suppose you do ... I've also heard that he has authority from the chief priests to arrest all those who call on your name. I'm not really, er, sure ...

JESUS

(Gently)

Ananias … Ananias … You must go for I have chosen him. I have chosen him to bear my name before the Gentiles, kings and the Children of Israel.

ANANIAS

(Seems very surprised)

I see, I see … goodness …

JESUS

And what's more, I will show him all the things that he must suffer for my name's sake. Now go.

ANANIAS

Yes Lord, yes. As you say Lord …

(Rises quickly and makes his way to the door. He goes to the house where PAUL is staying and calls at the door)

Hello! Hello to the house of Judas!

WOMAN SERVANT

One moment sir.

(Goes to the door and opens it to allow ANANIAS in)

PAUL

(Quietly and slowly)

Is there someone there?

WOMAN SERVANT

Yes my lord, a man …

PAUL

Hello there … you must be Ananias.

ANANIAS

… ah, yes, hello. Yes, I am Ananias.

(Slowly walks over to where PAUL is sitting and puts his hands on him)

My brother Paul …

PAUL

(PAUL raises his head in the direction of ANANIAS still unable to see)

ANANIAS

… the Lord Jesus, the one that appeared unto you as you made your way to Damascus. He has sent me that you might receive your sight and that you might be filled with the holy spirit.

(ANANIAS raises his head upwards)

In the name of Jesus Christ of Nazareth, I command that your sight be restored!

PAUL

(Gasps and stands up abruptly)

My eyes, my eyes - I can see. I can see! You are Ananias!

ANANIAS

Yes indeed I am!

PAUL

You, you .. are just as I saw you in the vision! Why it's as if scales have fallen away from my eyes. I can see!

(Becoming emotional)

It's like the precious ointment that ran over Aaron's beard. It's like the dew of Hermon on the mountains of Zion! God's blessing has been shown to me! Oh my Lord! Oh my Lord!

(He hugs ANANIAS and they both rejoice)

ANANIAS

Yes indeed Paul, without a doubt he is your Lord. The God of our fathers has chosen you that you should know his will and see the Just One and hear the voice of his mouth.

PAUL

I have heard, I have heard the voice of his mouth - on the road here!

ANANIAS

Paul, you shall be his witness and tell all men what you have seen and heard.

PAUL

He has shown me his grace! Blessed be the Lord out of Zion which dwells in Jerusalem! All praise be to him!

(Paces about the room and then stops abruptly and looks sadly at ANANIAS)

But Ananias ...

ANANIAS

Paul?

PAUL

How could I have been so wrong? What have I done?

ANANIAS

What do you mean Paul?

PAUL

Do you know why I was on the road to Damascus?

(ANANIAS quietly nods his head)

I had letters to bind all those who call on the name of Jesus Christ. I was going to throw them in prison!

(Paces about speaking)

If you only knew how often I've done that. I've chased men and women from city to city, caught them and forced them to deny Jesus Christ! Oh how could I have done that Ananias, how?

ANANIAS

Paul, you ...

PAUL

(Beginning to get more and more choked up as he speaks)

There was a family in Bethany ... two young children. The father ... well, he just refused to listen to me! We threw him in prison and the next day ... the next day ... I, ... I voted to put him to death ... oh Ananias, that poor, poor family, those children! They had done nothing wrong. Oh Lord, how could I have done such a thing? And then Stephen ... poor young Stephen ... I stood over his body and saw the blood flow down his innocent head. I've seen so many of your people beaten to the point of death ... my rage against them knew no bounds. Lord, where did I miss you in the ancient scrolls? Why could I not see you before? Oh Lord, - I was so ignorant before you, like a beast with eyes but could not see. I have been blind, so blind ... and ... much, much longer than these last three days. What a fool I have been!

(Starts to gently sob. Turns towards ANANIAS)

Ananias, is there forgiveness for a man like me? Am I to find any balm in Gilead?

ANANIAS

Paul, Paul, that I am here makes it clear that you have God's favor on your life. All men are ignorant until they know the Lord Jesus Christ.

(Takes PAUL by the shoulders)

You have been forgiven and given a new purpose by the Lord himself. He told me before I came that you are a chosen vessel to bear his name before the Gentiles, kings and the Children of Israel. Though he also told me that you must suffer for his sake, you must choose to serve him now with integrity of heart and conviction of soul. Do not tarry - know that your sins are forgiven and continue to call on the name of the Lord.

PAUL

A chosen vessel? It is almost too much to bear. Oh God, you are the Living God, you are steadfast for ever and of your dominion there shall be no end. There is none like you in all the earth. But who am I that you would choose me? I am the least of all - not worthy to be called by you ... but alas, you have shown me mercy. You have laid your merciful hand upon me. You have allowed me to see your son ... your son, my Lord ... so that I might know the purpose of your calling. You have opened my eyes O Lord ... eyes that have been closed far too long. You have called me by your grace and shown wisdom to an ignorant heart. The scales of darkness have been lifted from my eyes so that I can truly see and know the Just One that you have sent.

(Looks upwards)

I will serve the Lord, O God, I will serve him. I will serve him with all my heart. I will do my utmost to make his name known to the Gentiles, kings and my people, the Children of Israel. I will not turn from your calling. I will run the race ... that you have graciously set before me.

(BLACKOUT)

(END OF ACT 1)

ACT 2
Scene 1

SETTING: A market in Lystra several years later.

AT RISE: PAUL and BARNABAS walk along the road. They are speaking as they walk. A CRIPPLE is sitting just ahead of them in the market.

NARRATOR

After Paul was personally called by Jesus Christ to make known the gospel, he immediately began to preach Christ at every opportunity. He spent three years in Arabia and some time at home in Tarsus to reflect and consult the Scriptures and was eventually accepted by the church in Judea. After spending more than a year in Jerusalem, God sent Paul and Barnabas on Paul's first journey to spread the gospel. After many adventures, they arrive in Lystra.

BARNABAS

(They stop to drink some water and rest)

Looks like Lystra is just ahead Paul.

PAUL

Let's hope the welcome is better here than our departure from
Antioch and Iconium.

BARNABAS

It was a close call at Iconium.

PAUL

Seems some of the more devout Jewish brothers are intent on
preventing the message of the Christ from being heard.

BARNABAS

They certainly seemed to organize very quickly - especially after
the Gentiles started showing interest. They were on us faster than
women around a groom at a Jewish wedding.

PAUL

(PAUL laughs)

Yes, but for very different reasons ...

(He pauses and looks back)

BARNABAS

What is it Paul? Still thinking about John Mark?

PAUL

Hmm - yes. How did you guess?

BARNABAS

It was a sad parting at Perga - totally unexpected. Maybe he was a little troubled at the sorcerer from Paphos being made blind. Maybe it had something to do with that rough voyage from Paphos or that pirate ship we saw in the distance. He did look a little worried.

PAUL

Hmm - possibly. Maybe all those stories of Alexander and the Pisidian Highlanders filled him with fear. It was no easy journey to Iconium, that's for sure.

BARNABAS

No it wasn't. If I'm honest, I thought a little about some of the stories I've heard myself.

PAUL

Thankfully the Lord was steadfast in his protection. I pray Mark is safe in Jerusalem.

(They start to walk towards the man by the market)

CROWD MEMBER 3

Welcome travelers - come and enjoy some food and drink.

BARNABAS

Greetings good sir - we are grateful for your hospitality.

CROWD MEMBER 3

Looks like you have traveled from Iconium.

BARNABAS

Yes but our journey started in Antioch of Syria.

PRIEST OF ZEUS

You have come a long way - welcome friends. Do you bring a message for us?

BARNABAS

(Bows to the priest and looks at PAUL)

PAUL

Friends and citizens of Lystra - gather around. We bring you tidings of great joy. God, the creator of heaven and earth - he is the one that gives life and breath to everyone.

(Some talking in the crowd)

PRIEST OF ZEUS

Quiet everyone - pay heed to our travelers! Go on good sir.

PAUL

Because he gives life and breath to all, you cannot make an image of him from gold, or silver or stone. There was a time when people did this and God has graciously ignored their ignorance of him.

CRIPPLE

(Starts to look intently at PAUL)

PAUL

God has never left himself without witness. Why everyone, even by looking around at his creation should recognize the handiwork of the Almighty God - his eternal power is obvious. Man is without excuse. This same God who made the heaven and earth has declared that all men must repent and believe on that man whom he hath sent. That man is his son, Jesus Christ.

(General murmuring in the crowd. The CRIPPLE continues to stare at PAUL)

And what did God do so that no one could miss his great purpose? After Jesus had been crucified and lain in the grave for three days and three nights - God raised him from the dead!

(Gasps from the crowd)

And now he asks all men to believe on the name of his son, Jesus Christ.

CRIPPLE

I believe you good sir! I believe you!

PAUL

Whosoever believes on the name of Jesus Christ shall never be disappointed. When Jesus was here, God had anointed him with the holy spirit and power. As a result he did much good and healed all those who were oppressed by the devil.

CRIPPLE

Did you say healed? Can that be?

PAUL

(Looking at the crippled man)

Yes brother .. the same Jesus that God raised from the dead declared that in his name the sick would be healed.

CRIPPLE

Even from a condition such as mine?

PAUL

There is nothing that is too hard for the Lord. Do you believe that you can be healed by the power of the Almighty God?

CRIPPLE

Yes, yes! Oh yes, I do!

PAUL

Do you believe that if I call on the name of his son now, you will be healed?

CRIPPLE

Oh yes I do! I believe on the name of Jesus Christ with all my heart!

PAUL

(In a loud voice)

In the name of Jesus Christ, stand up on your feet!

CRIPPLE

(Leaps up and starts walking around. CROWD starts shouting)

I can walk! I can walk!

CROWD MEMBER 4

(Speaking in their own language, lots of shouting and noise)

Yeshtuka - gina baloke! Zus! Hermis! Yani, yani - neestrom undava!

PRIEST OF ZEUS

Bindama nuni - Findasto - neestrom undava! Neestrom comos Zus soma Hermis!

BARNABAS

(To CROWD MEMBER 5)

What are they saying?

CROWD MEMBER 5

(Kneeling down before PAUL and BARNABAS but not looking directly at them out of fear)

They say that you are gods who have come as men to visit us. Praise to you! Praise be to you!

PRIEST OF ZEUS

(Looking at BARNABAS)

All hail to you Zeus!

(Crowd shouts in agreement, the PRIEST OF ZEUS turns to PAUL)

All hail to you Hermes! Bring the oxen and the garlands ... we must hold a sacrifice now! Let us celebrate this great event! The gods have come down to us!

CROWD MEMBER 4

All hail Zeus! All hail Hermes! Praise be to the gods!

PAUL

No! No! What are you doing?

BARNABAS

You must not do this! We are men just like you!

PAUL

You must stop this very moment! We do not want your sacrifices.

PRIEST OF ZEUS

But it is only right that we should honor a visit by the gods.

PAUL

We are not gods. We are men - the same as all of you. We ask that you turn from these vain practices to the Living God. It is he who made heaven, the earth and the sea - and everything that is in the sea. It was not these gods that you worship.

CROWD MEMBER 5

(Astonished by his words)

What?? What is he saying?

PAUL

In past generations, God allowed the nations to do as they pleased - to walk in their own ways. But even then … even then he did good things for all nations - by sending rain from heaven, plenteous harvests and filling men's hearts with food and gladness. So you must stop with these sacrifices to them that are no gods - but the work of men's hands.

PRIEST OF ZEUS

But the sacrifices …

CROWD MEMBER 3

(CROWD murmurs in agreement)

Yes, yes - the sacrifices!

BARNABAS

No, you must not do this! You must worship the One True God, the Living God - and not these false gods of stone and wood. You cannot do this sacrifice.

(Two JEWISH MEN now step forward from the crowd)

JEWISH MAN 1

Hail, Priest of Zeus and fellow citizens!

PRIEST OF ZEUS

Welcome travelers. Do you have a message for us as well?

JEWISH MAN 2

Yes we do - we are here to call out these two imposters!

(Pointing at PAUL and BARNABAS)

CROWD MEMBER 4

(General murmuring)

What … what is going on?

CRIPPLE

But they made me walk. I was healed by them!

JEWISH MAN 1

Oh yes, they are quite accomplished at magic tricks - just like the sorcerer of Paphos who is their friend! They use their trickery to deceive all that they meet.

PAUL

These are lies!

BARNABAS

There is no truth to what he is saying! Like the sorcerer at Paphos, these men are attempting to obstruct the good news of Jesus Christ.

JEWISH MAN 2

Of course they will deny it. Tell me, good priest, have they not just tried to stop you from carrying out the worship of your gods that you have been doing for countless years?

PRIEST OF ZEUS

Well, yes, it is true, that is what they suggested.

JEWISH MAN 1

See! I warned you - they are deceivers bent on changing your customs and traditions so they can steal your fortunes.

(To the CRIPPLE)

And do you think that they will not ask for payment for their magic tricks?

CROWD MEMBER 4

(Starting to get restless)

Is this true? Could this be true?

JEWISH MAN 2

Do you even know who they are? How dare strangers try and change the worship that your people have always relied on? They say their God has given you rain and a good harvest - how can they prove that?

CROWD MEMBER 4

(Looking at PAUL and BARNABAS)

Yes ... tell us, how? How do we know that is true?

JEWISH MAN 2

What about Demeter? Do not the seasons and the harvest flow from her good graces?

PRIEST OF ZEUS

Yes that is true ... you speak the truth indeed.

PAUL

These are falsehoods. These men are Judeans - they do not even believe in Demeter themselves. These are lies to turn you away from the Almighty God who made heaven and earth.

JEWISH MAN 1

Silence! You've done enough damage to these good people. They have been nothing but kind and you have repaid them with falsehoods! Have you no shame?!

JEWISH MAN 2

(To the crowd and pointing at PAUL)

Why do you allow this to go on any further? This man must not be allowed to live! He has disgraced your priest and all that you believe with his clever words!

CROWD MEMBER 3

Yes, yes - he was doing most of the talking! How foolish we have been.

CRIPPLE

But this is not true …

JEWISH MAN 1

(Pushes the CRIPPLE aside)

Well, what are you waiting for? The Roman punishment for those who subvert your beliefs is death! Will you defy the Roman government as well?

CROWD MEMBER 4

No, no - this man speaks the truth.

(Pointing at PAUL)

Away with him!

PRIEST OF ZEUS

Take him over there against that wall.

PAUL

Sir … these men are Judeans. They have no interest …

PRIEST OF ZEUS

I've heard enough! Silence! You have said enough, by the power of Zeus, I condemn you to death by stoning! Citizens!

BARNABAS

No! You must not.

(The two JEWISH MEN grab BARNABAS and take him aside and a few others drag him away shouting)

CROWD MEMBER 4

(Some of the crowd start to pick up stones, others back away)

Shut him up now!

JEWISH MAN 1

Justice for Lystra! Justice for Lystra!

JEWISH MAN 2

All hail Zeus! And may Caesar be honored!

PRIEST OF ZEUS

Citizens! He is in your hands!

CROWD MEMBER 3

(They start to stone PAUL)

Trickster! Liar! Charlatan! Where is your God now?

PAUL

(Falls to the ground after being hit by a few stones)

Help me God … ahhhh!

CROWD MEMBER 4

(Continues shouting and throwing stones encouraged by the JEWISH MEN)

Hit him again! Don't let him up!

PRIEST OF ZEUS

Praise be to Zeus!

PAUL

(Lies still. The JEWISH MEN slowly skulk away from the crowd and disappear)

CROWD MEMBER 5

I think he's dead! I think we got him. OK, he's done!

PRIEST OF ZEUS

Away to your homes now and pay homage to Zeus for his goodness.

CROWD MEMBER 3

Yes, Praise be to Zeus.

(The PRIEST OF ZEUS and most of the crowd leave PAUL lying there. The CRIPPLE and a few others remain behind and approach PAUL. BARNABAS also returns)

BARNABAS

Paul! Paul!

(Kneels down and holds PAUL)

Oh it cannot be - he is not breathing!

CRIPPLE

Are you sure?

BARNABAS

Yes, quite sure. Listen to me everyone. Come around please, gather round.

(BARNABAS stands up, the CRIPPLE and others stand around the limp form of PAUL)

BARNABAS

(Looks upwards)

Lord, you are the God of heaven and earth - our times are in your hands. God, hear us now as we lift up our prayer to you on behalf of our brother Paul.

(They stand silently for a few seconds. BARNABAS addresses PAUL'S body - in a loud voice)

In the name of Jesus Christ, get up!

PAUL

(Starts to stir)

Ohh ... where am I? What happened?

CRIPPLE

He's alive! He's alive! Praise be to the God of heaven and earth!

CROWD MEMBER 6

A miracle! He is alive!

BARNABAS

Oh thank you Father, thank you.

CRIPPLE

He is the True God. He is the God of gods!

PAUL

(Sits up. Reaches up to the CRIPPLE'S hand. The CRIPPLE pulls him up)

Well, we have seen many things today - by the grace of Almighty God and the Lord Jesus Christ.

BARNABAS

Yes, yes, we certainly have. You had us worried for a moment, my brother.

PAUL

(Smiling rather seriously)

My last thoughts were of Stephen.

BARNABAS

Hmm.

CRIPPLE

Good sirs - might I be so forward as to impose on you one thing further?

PAUL

Yes?

CRIPPLE

Would you be so kind as to lodge in my humble abode this evening for the day is far spent. You are in need of rest.

PAUL

We would be very grateful for the lodging - for we must depart on the morrow for Derbe. The gospel must be preached there next.

CRIPPLE

I am pleased ... but there is one thing more.

BARNABAS

Say on brother.

CRIPPLE

Could you please speak more to me about your God?

PAUL

(Pats him on the back)

Our God brother, Our God.

(BLACKOUT)

(END OF SCENE)

ACT 2
Scene 2

SETTING: In the city of Troas.

AT RISE: PAUL, SILAS and TIMOTHY are standing in an open area. The night air is chilly.

NARRATOR

After the first journey that Paul took, he returned to Antioch of Syria. On his next journey, Paul chose Silas as one of his companions and revisited some of the places that he had previously been. During their journey, a young man named Timothy joined them. Paul and company eventually reached Troas.

SILAS

(Trying to stay warm)

It's rather damp here, don't you think?

PAUL

Yes, the wind off the sea isn't helping matters. Let's build a fire. Timothy, see about getting some wood together. Silas and I will prepare the ground.

TIMOTHY

(Also shivering)

Yes Paul - a very good idea.

SILAS

(After TIMOTHY has wandered off a bit)

Remarkable young man, isn't he?

PAUL

Yes. At such a young age - already committed to the gospel. There are few like him. Comes from a faithful family - both his mother Eunice and his grandmother Lois - full of genuine faith.

SILAS

It seems he has inherited much of that - if that is even possible.

PAUL

Yes, if only. In fact his father is a Gentile. The decision to follow the Lord was clearly his and his alone - though his mother and grandmother's teaching has found it's way into his heart.

TIMOTHY

(Returns with some wood)

Not only am I cold but I'm a little hungry too.

SILAS

Cold **and** hungry? Well, well. Don't you know young man, those are actually benefits when you travel with Paul?

(SILAS and PAUL laugh)

And if you pay extra, you might even be party to a stoning!

TIMOTHY

(To PAUL)

My parents told me about your stoning when you were in Lystra for the first time. They said it was a miracle that you were raised from the dead.

PAUL

God's abounding grace on my life, my son. I certainly had nothing to do with it.

SILAS

Thanks be to God for his grace Paul.

TIMOTHY

And as far as getting stoned goes Master Silas, after being circumcised in Lystra, I think that I could handle it!

(PAUL and SILAS both laugh)

SILAS

Still a little tender Timotheus?

TIMOTHY

What was all that about Master Paul? You never did explain it to me? I do know that you and Master Silas were teaching that it was no longer a requirement of God.

PAUL

You are correct. The Law of Moses was fulfilled by the work of our Lord Jesus Christ and circumcision is no longer a requirement. It was not for the sake of any requirement before God, Timothy, but only a precaution. The Judean legalists had eyes everywhere - all they needed was an excuse. We were not going to give them one. They were the same group responsible for the stoning on my previous visit and they know your father.

TIMOTHY

Yes of course Master Paul - though I must admit they were not the most comfortable three days that I have spent.

SILAS

(Laughs)

Cold, sore and hungry - hey young man?!

TIMOTHY

Now I know why Simeon and Levi faced no opposition when they attacked Shalem after all the men were circumcised.

(SILAS and PAUL both laugh)

PAUL

Why don't the both of you gather some more wood and I will prepare the supper?

SILAS

(Smiling at PAUL)

Come on Timothy .. if you are able?

TIMOTHY

(Walks off with SILAS)

PAUL

(PAUL attends the fire and a man appears in a mist above where PAUL is sitting)

Hello? Who goes there?

MAN OF MACEDONIA

Please, please come to Macedonia.

PAUL

(Realizing it is a vision)

Oh ...

MAN OF MACEDONIA

Please, please come to Macedonia and help us.

(The man disappears)

PAUL

Silas! Timothy! Come quick! Come quick!

(They appear with more wood)

SILAS

What is it Paul? Are you alright?

PAUL

Yes, yes - the Lord has just sent us a message.

TIMOTHY

What Master Paul?

PAUL

We are to go to Macedonia - they are in need of our assistance.

SILAS

But where in Macedonia Paul?

PAUL

We will leave at first light - I am quite sure details will follow. The Lord will never leave or forsake us. Let's eat and get our rest ... the race continues tomorrow.

(BLACKOUT)

(END OF SCENE)

ACT 2

Scene 3

SETTING: In the city of Philippi (Macedonia).

AT RISE: PAUL, SILAS and TIMOTHY are at the house of LYDIA. They are gathered in a room with three other women. PAUL and SILAS are off to the side speaking quietly.

TIMOTHY

(To LYDIA)

We are ever so grateful for your kind hospitality.

LYDIA

Not at all, the joy and pleasure has been ours - to think that we would have the blessing to meet the servants of the Lord - right here in our city. What made you come to the river?

TIMOTHY

It has been Master Paul's manner to first visit the synagogues. We are well aware that Philippi is a colonia and there is no synagogue here. Upon entering the city we were made aware that there was a prayer gathering near the river so we went.

SARAH

It was so fortunate for us that you did.

REBECCA

What led you to our city in the first place?

TIMOTHY

Not so much fortune but the mercy of our Lord God. He showed Master Paul a vision - a man of Macedonia asking for assistance. We wasted no time in making our way here from Troas.

SARAH

Have you met this man?

TIMOTHY

(Looking at the three ladies around him)

Hmm .. well ...

(They all laugh)

PAUL

(Laughs also)

God himself told Moses to wait and see if his Word would come to pass or not. We do the same.

LYDIA

Is everyone ready to go to prayer?

TIMOTHY

Master Paul and Master Silas will be joining you today - I've been given some chores to do in the city. I will join up with you later - same location?

LYDIA

Yes, by the river.

TIMOTHY

(TIMOTHY leaves)

LYDIA

Alright everyone, let's be on our way.

(They walk out the door)

SILAS

(Looking down the street where a crowd has gathered)

Paul, look! I believe it is that same woman that has been following us around.

PAUL

Yes, indeed it is.

LYDIA

Shall we take another street?

PAUL

No, it is time.

LYDIA

Time for what?

(SILAS takes her by the arm and shakes his head)

SALOME

(Sarcastically)

There they are again. Aren't they so wonderful?

(She points at PAUL and SILAS)

These men are the servants of the most high God!

PAUL

(Stops in front of the woman)

SALOME

(Circling around PAUL)

They are the ones who will show us the way of salvation. They are the servants of the most high God.

PAUL

Stand still woman!

SALOME

(More sarcastically and in a crazed manner)

Show me the way of salvation! You are the servant of the most high God! Show me the way of salvation!

PAUL

(Louder)

Stand still!

SALOME

(SALOME stops in her tracks looking right at PAUL)

PAUL

I command you in the name of Jesus Christ to come out of her!

SALOME

(Shrieks and falls to the ground moaning)

SILAS

(Walks over and takes her by the hand to help her up)

SALOME

(Quietly. Voice has noticeably changed)

Where am I? How did I get here? And ... and, why do I feel so at peace?

PAUL

Good lady, you have been delivered by the power of Jesus Christ. God has enabled all those who believe in Jesus Christ to walk in his power and ...

FELONIUS

(Steps in and cuts PAUL off. Takes SALOME by the shoulders)

What have you done? Salome! Salome! Where have you gone? What has happened to you?

BARAK

(Pushes PAUL away)

Stand aside you huckster! What sort of curse is this?!!

FELONIUS

Speak Salome - speak to us as you always have ... The crowd is waiting for you.

CROWD MEMBER 7

I have already paid you! She must do her job!

CROWD MEMBER 8

I have also - I want my money back! You scoundrel!

BARAK

Don't be so hasty my good men - Salome will be back.

(To SALOME harshly, holding her by the arm)

Speak now you hag or there will be no more food for your family! Speak!

SALOME

I do not understand. What is it you want me to say? I must go home at once.

(She breaks free with help from SILAS and runs off)

PAUL

Lydia, please follow her and tell her about the savior. She must understand her deliverance.

LYDIA

Come Rebecca, Rachel - we must go.

(They follow SALOME)

FELONIUS

(A crowd has gathered. The MAGISTRATE with his two AIDES is among them. To PAUL)

What is this you bring to our good city? You have destroyed our livelihood with your curses!

BARAK

(To a couple of men in the crowd)

Quickly - grab them before they escape!

CROWD MEMBER 7   CROWD MEMBER 8

(The men take hold of PAUL and SILAS)

MAGISTRATE

What is this commotion? Do I need to call the guards? Why the disturbance? This is a violation of Roman law.

FELONIUS

It is these strangers good magistrate - they are barbarians, Jews who trouble our city.

BARAK

They have no respect for Roman law!

CROWD MEMBER 7

I have heard them in the marketplace. They speak about another king and deny Caesar.

FELONIUS

They have been teaching customs that are unlawful for good Romans. They have even cursed Salome and stolen her living!

CROWD MEMBER 8

(Growing restless start to shout at PAUL and SILAS)

Get out you foreigners! Rome has no love for Jews!

MAGISTRATE

(To PAUL and SILAS)

Is this true?

PAUL

We have done nothing contrary to Roman law.

FELONIUS

Liar! Surely you are well aware that Roman law forbids foreign religions?

PAUL

But we ...

MAGISTRATE

Silence Jew!

(Rips his own tunic in disgust)

The emperor has banished your kind from Rome - as you well know. Philippi will not lose its status as a colonia by suffering your kind to destroy our laws and the livelihood of our good citizens.

CROWD MEMBER 7

Away with them magistrate! They must not be allowed to live!

BARAK

(To the CROWD)

Salome was your good servant and now she has been cursed! Her power is no more!

FELONIUS

Who will give you the revelation of the gods now?

CROWD MEMBER 8

They must be punished! Filthy Judeans!

FELONIUS

(To the MAGISTRATE)

Will you be a friend of Caesar or will you join in their duplicity?

CROWD MEMBER 7

Caesar! Caesar!

MAGISTRATE

(To his AIDES)

Take off their robes and scourge them now!

CROWD MEMBER 8

(Cheers)

Caesar! Caesar!

SILAS

But Roman law ...

MAGISTRATE

(With face glowing with anger)

Quiet! You who break the law dare teach me?! Lictors now!

AIDE 1   AIDE 2

(Strip off PAUL and SILAS'S robes, throw them to the ground and commence beating them)

CROWD MEMBER 7

Serves them right! Get out of Philippi vermin!

AIDE 1   AIDE 2

(They continue the beating until they are both bleeding)

MAGISTRATE

To the prison now!

(The AIDES grab them, force them up and take them away to the jail)

CROWD MEMBER 7   CROWD MEMBER 8

(Cheer)

Away with you! Hail Caesar!

FELONIUS

Ruin our business, will you ... seems that Rome is just a little more powerful than your Judean God ...

(BLACKOUT)

(END OF SCENE)

ACT 2

Scene 4

SETTING: In a jail in the city of Philippi.

AT RISE: PAUL and SILAS are blood stained and being held in stocks. The JAILOR is standing outside the cell. The jail has no windows and is dirty with rats. There are a couple of other prisoners sleeping in an adjacent cell. There is a single candle burning in the jail.

JAILOR

(Leaving the cell)

Maybe this will teach you not to defy Roman law. If the jail doesn't, the rats will.

(Laughs, blows out the candle and exits)

PAUL

(Weakly)

I pray that Lydia and the household are at peace.

SILAS

And the new girl ...

PAUL

Yes, she will have much to forget and much to learn.

(Looking upwards)

In your good mercy O God, we pray for Lydia and her household. May you keep them safe. May you give them wisdom in helping the slave girl so that her deliverance from the evil one is complete. We ask for your watchful care over their lives and ours. May you keep us all in your hands.

(Pauses)

Silas?

SILAS

Yes Paul?

PAUL

Do you recall that Psalm that Timothy always seems to be singing?

SILAS

Hmm. Yes, yes I do, didn't he say that Lois, his grandmother taught it to him when he was a boy?

PAUL

Yes, yes, that is the one. Do you think that the other prisoners might know it?

SILAS

No, but somehow I believe that they are going to learn.

PAUL

(Starts to sing slowly and quietly)

My times are in thy hands, O Lord

(Coughs, pauses, winces a bit due to the pain)

(SILAS starts to sing with him)

PAUL   SILAS

(Singing together)

My times are in thy hands.

Thou, my rock, my fortress
Guide me for thy sake
From my enemies save me
My life let them not take

(The other prisoners hear the singing and wake up. They stir and start to listen intently. PAUL and SILAS get a little louder)

My times are in thy hands, O Lord
My times are in thy hands

Fear on every side my God
Words to break my heart
But I trust in thee, O Lord
Let lying lips depart

(PAUL and SILAS now quite forcefully)

My times are in thy hands, O Lord
My times are in thy hands

Love the Lord all ye his saints
Let your pride be cast aside
For all who find their hope in him
In his presence will abide

My times are in thy hands, O Lord
My times are in thy hands

(There is a very large and intense rumble as an earthquake hits and shakes the jail. They keep singing)

My times are in thy hands, O Lord
My times are in thy hands

(The rumble stops and the cell doors fly open. The JAILOR appears suddenly but it is still dark)

JAILOR

Whaaa .... t .. the cell doors! All open ... oh no ... What has happened?
And on my watch... I have let them escape ...

(Draws out his sword and is about to kill himself)

PAUL

No! You must not do that! Do not harm yourself - we are all here sir! Put your sword away.

JAILOR

What? What did you say?

(Calls to someone behind him)

Boy, get some lights to me now! Quickly!

AIDE 1

(Appears and hands him a candle)

SILAS

We are all here good sir!

JAILOR

How were the doors opened? Where are your accomplices?

SILAS

No sir, there are none - just us, we are all here.

JAILOR

(Visibly shaken)

I do not understand ... I did not see anyone ... how did this happen?

PAUL

The one who has done this you cannot see.

JAILOR

Wha...???

PAUL

Tell me sir, what is your name?

JAILOR

(Trembling)

Ru ... fus ... uhh .. Rufus.

PAUL

Rufus, my brother Silas and I have been doing nothing but praying and singing praises to the God who created the heaven and the earth. He has seen fit in his mercy to deliver us by sending an earthquake.

JAILOR

(Looking intently at PAUL. The other prisoners also watch PAUL closely)

I ... I see ...

PAUL

The God of heaven that no man has seen is our father. In times past he has made himself known by his creation, his miraculous acts and the voices of the prophets. There is no man on the earth who can have an excuse to not know the One True God. It is God who has made known unto us the way of salvation.

JAILOR

(Falling to his knees - very moved and still trembling - looking at both PAUL and SILAS)

Wh...whaa ... what must I do to be saved?

PAUL

In these recent times Rufus, that same God has spoken to us by way of his son, the Lord Jesus Christ. It is Jesus who he has ordained to be the judge of the living and the dead. It is Jesus who he has marked as the one in whom everyone must believe ... and God did this by raising his son, Jesus, from the dead. He has said that there is salvation in no other name but the name of Jesus. Everyone without exception must believe on the name of Jesus Christ. There is no other name given under heaven by which anyone can be saved.

JAILOR

Yes, yes ... I understand. I have heard of this Jesus of whom you speak.

SILAS

Do you believe Rufus, do you believe on him?

JAILOR

(Sobbing quietly)

Yes ... yes... I do. Oh yes I do ... please help me ...

PAUL

Do you believe that Jesus is your Lord?

JAILOR

(Starting to get more convicted)

Yes sir ... I do believe.

SILAS

Do you believe that God has raised him from the dead?

JAILOR

(Stands up ... now very excited)

Yes! Yes! I believe on him! Oh yes I do - I believe on the name of Jesus Christ!

PAUL

By the Word of God Rufus, you have been saved. You are a child of the Living God!

JAILOR

Oh thanksgiving and praise be to God! Please brothers, I beg you to come to my house so that my family can hear your words! Please, please, I beg you.

(Holding PAUL'S arm)

PAUL

Yes of course.

JAILOR

It is nearby and I will get my wife Sarah to clean your wounds. And yes, you must eat with us ... how hungry you must be! You must meet my children ... they need to hear ... oh how wonderful! Praises be to God!

JAILOR

Please wait here ... I will let my assistant know that you are under my authority .. and then we will depart.

(Closes the cell doors)

Please .. just stay right there .... praises be to God!

SILAS

(Prisoners are gesturing towards SILAS as if they want to hear more)

Yes, yes we will return and speak with you ... they have not released us. We will make some time when we are back ... I promise ...

(The prisoners seem relieved)

Paul?

PAUL

Yes Silas?

SILAS

The man? The man in the vision at Troas?!

PAUL

(Smiles)

SILAS

It was him. It was Rufus … wasn't it?

PAUL

His word will always surely come to pass. In his great mercy Silas … our times are truly in his hands …

(BLACKOUT)

(END OF ACT 2)

ACT 3
Scene 1

SETTING: In the house of PHILIP the evangelist at Caesarea. Several years later.

AT RISE: LUKE is standing beside a table with PHILIP. PHILIP's four daughters are sitting at the table.

NARRATOR

During Paul's third journey, he again visited the churches and spent about two years in Ephesus. After traveling through Macedonia and Greece, he made his way towards Judea and received several warnings from God to not go back to Jerusalem. One of these he received in Caesarea at the house of Philip the evangelist about seventy miles from Jerusalem. Luke was with Paul at this time.

PHILIP

That was some journey Luke, you've certainly seen your share of troubles and blessings all at the same time.

LUKE

Yes you could say that, there is no question that Paul is single minded in the race that our Lord has set before him. But then again my brother, you are hardly a stranger to these matters. You've done much for the ministry of the gospel. People still talk about what you did in Samaria to this day.

RUTH

Yes Father, please tell us about Samaria again! Oh please!

RACHEL

And about the healing Father - those evil spirits, the lame ...

ELIZABETH

And that evil sorcerer .. what did he say again?

MARY

Oh yes, and about that Egyptian prince Father! Please!

(All the daughters start asking)

PHILIP

Girls, girls please! Stop ... please ... all this commotion!

(LUKE begins to laugh)

This is hardly the time - our visitors are tired and need to rest. They have come on a long journey. I wager if you were to speak to Master Luke, you might be able to persuade him to tell you a story or two about their journeys.

RUTH   MARY   RACHEL   ELIZABETH

(All speaking at once)

Yes ... Master Luke .. will you? Will you please!

LUKE

Well ...

PHILIP

Not right now girls ... oh heavens ... go now and help your mother prepare the food for our guests. Out with you now!

RUTH   MARY   RACHEL   ELIZABETH

(All together)

O Father ....

PHILIP

(Sternly)

Girls.

RUTH   MARY   RACHEL   ELIZABETH

(Once again ... all speaking)

OK Father ... but later on, please Master Luke?

LUKE

Of course girls we will talk.

(They leave the room reluctantly)

Oh, you are a blessed man - such joy in this house!

PHILIP

Joy? All this chattering - a heritage of the Lord? - tired is the man that has his quiver full of them!

(PHILIP and LUKE laugh)

PHILIP

But you are right ... they are the joy of my life.

LUKE

Not just that - the prophecies they gave earlier shows a keen walk with the master. You've taught them well Philip - there is no doubt of that.

PHILIP

You are kind.

LUKE

The words spoken were an encouragement for all of us to continue to obey our God without doubting. What great messages!

(PHILIP nods with thankfulness. PAUL enters)

PAUL

What was all the noise about?

PHILIP

Oh just some memories of many years ago Paul and some rather over zealous daughters.

PAUL

Your daughters are a credit to you.

PHILIP

Thank you - their mother and I are very thankful. Usually very tired - but at the same time very thankful.

(PAUL and LUKE laugh)

PHILIP

(There is a knock at the door)

Paul, I've invited a few of the brothers to our meal today. I hope that is agreeable to you.

PAUL

Yes of course, as generous as always - I am not the least bit surprised.

PHILIP

(Opens the door and welcomes three men)

Ahh .. welcome, welcome brethren. Come and sit with us, we will break bread together shortly.

(The visitors greet LUKE and PAUL with hugs)

LUKE

Hello brothers. Welcome.

PAUL

Welcome, welcome ... God's blessings be upon you.

VISITOR 1

And on you Master Paul, Master Luke.

VISITOR 2

We have heard much of your travels and the miracles among the Gentiles. Will you share about your journeys?

PAUL

Yes, yes .. certainly ... God has shown us much grace and opened many doors.

(PHILIP'S daughters return carrying some plates of food and set them on the table)

PHILIP

That's wonderful girls.

VISITOR 3

Hello ladies. Blessings be upon Philip's beautiful daughters.

(And gently to RUTH)

Hello Ruth ...

MARY   RACHEL

(Sheepishly at RUTH)

Ooooo ...

RUTH

Be quiet you two!

(To the young man)

Hello ...

PHILIP

Everyone, let us sit and break bread ... Luke, if you would be so kind as to give thanks?

LUKE

Certainly ....

(As he is about to pray, there is a loud knock at the door)

PHILIP

Well, who could that be? I have not invited anyone else.

AGABUS

(From outside the door)

Greetings to the house of Philip. I come in the name of the Lord.

PHILIP

(Opens the door)

Ah Agabus, welcome and God's blessings be upon you. What brings you all the way from Judea to my humble home?

AGABUS

Blessings upon your home Philip.

PHILIP

Might I ask you to join us Agabus - we are about to break bread together. You must be tired from your journey.

AGABUS

Thank you for your kind invitation - but the Lord's business must come first. I bring a message for Paul.

PAUL

(Rising from the table)

Greetings Agabus.

AGABUS

Paul, the good Lord has seen fit to send you a message.

(Takes PAUL'S sash/tunic from his waist. He sits on the floor and ties his own hands and feet with the sash. The others look on with bewilderment)

Thus has God spoken. In this manner will the Jews at Jerusalem bind the man who owns this tunic and they will then deliver him to the Gentiles!

LUKE

Paul, you must not go to Jerusalem. Agabus speaks by the word of the Lord.

PHILIP

Luke is correct Paul, God's will is clear. He has sent Agabus all the way from Judea to deliver this message. You must not go.

LUKE

While we were on our way here, at Miletus, didn't you say that you felt bound in the spirit? You said that God had shown you that you might end up bound and beaten. Please listen to Agabus, you should not go to Jerusalem.

PAUL

Yes Luke .. but ..

RACHEL

Uncle Paul, we do not want any harm to come to you.

MARY

Please do not go.

RUTH   ELIZABETH

You mustn't go!

LUKE

There will be another time Paul.

PHILIP

Surely the message is clear Paul. You must not go to Jerusalem.

PAUL

(Agitated)

What are you all trying to do? Why are you crying on my behalf?
Why are you trying to break my heart? Don't you know, don't you
understand that I am ready for anything. If I get bound, then I get
bound!

LUKE

But the message Paul. Do you recall in the early days when Agabus
told us of the coming famine? He was correct – it came to pass as he
had prophesied. He is a prophet of the Lord ... God's will has been
made known ... and more than once!

PAUL

Surely you know by now. I don't care if I am taken prisoner. In fact,
I am ready to die in Jerusalem for the name of the Lord Jesus!

PHILIP

Brother, I know your great love for Israel, your nation, your great desire for their salvation ... but certainly not at the expense of your safety.

PAUL

I must go Philip ... it is clear to me that I must go.

LUKE

God would not have sent Agabus all this way to warn you if it was not important Paul.

PAUL

I must go Luke. I will go and see about the preparations for the journey up to Jerusalem. We leave in a few days.

(Leaves the room. The room is quiet for a moment)

PHILIP

Agabus? What can we do?

AGABUS

I have spoken the Word of the Lord. God's will has been made known. We can do no more.

RUTH

Father?

PHILIP

Girls, your Uncle Paul will need much prayer.

LUKE

Let us all pray that Paul's race does not end in Jerusalem.

(BLACKOUT)

(END OF SCENE)

ACT 3

Scene 2

SETTING: A Roman court in Caesarea.

AT RISE: PAUL is sitting by himself. FELIX is officiating
             over the proceedings with the guards standing
             near him. The elders and TERTULLUS are
             seated before FELIX. A few others are seated
             in the back. Everyone is speaking among
             themselves.

NARRATOR

Despite God's warnings, Paul and company did end up going
to Jerusalem after their visit to Philip's house. As Agabus had
prophesied, Paul was captured by the Romans and imprisoned in
Jerusalem. He was later sent to Caesarea to appear before Felix, the
Roman governor.

FELIX

Citizens, I ask for your silence please. Quiet everyone ... quiet.

(Pauses while waiting for them to quiet down)

In the name of Caesar, I commence with the proceeding before us. I believe that you, Citizen Tertullus, will be speaking on behalf of the Jews against the accused? I hereby give you license to begin.

TERTULLUS

(Stands up before the group)

Many thanks most excellent Governor Felix.

(With obvious attempts at praise)

And might I say that it is by your good grace that we enjoy such peace in our districts. And indeed it is by your excellent foresight that many reforms are being done for our nation.

FELIX

(Getting a little annoyed)

Yes ... yes ... proceed.

TERTULLUS

In every way and everywhere we humbly accept this with all gratitude. But, I know you are a busy man so I will detain you no further. I beg you to kindly hear our brief case.

FELIX

The floor is yours. Proceed.

TERTULLUS

(Points at PAUL)

This man is a plague to our nation! First, he has been traveling far and wide to cause disturbance and stir up riots among our people. Surely this is a treasonous act against the Emperor himself!

ELDER 1

(General mumbling in agreement among the ELDERS)

Yes ... yes ... treason ... yes!

TERTULLUS

Second, he has proven himself to be a ringleader of the sect that follows the Nazarene!

ELDER 2

Heresy! Heresy against Moses! We have seen his heresy!

FELIX

Silence please, silence!

TERTULLUS

Third, he was even found trying to profane our temple! It was our good fortune that we were able to stop him. If you examine him yourself, you will see that every accusation that we are making is indeed the truth.

ELDER 1

True .. they are all true. We have seen it ourselves. Tertullus speaks the truth!

FELIX

Silence everyone! Are you finished?

TERTULLUS

(Bows to FELIX)

Yes your grace. There is nothing more to say. I believe that the evidence is clear.

FELIX

Paul the prisoner ... please stand up...

PAUL

(Rising to his feet)

FELIX

I give you license to make your own defense. You may begin ... silence everyone.

PAUL

Though I do know, sir, that you are a judge to this nation, I am thankful to have the opportunity to give an answer to the accusations that have been laid against me.

FELIX

(Nods)

PAUL

It has only been about 12 days that I came to Jerusalem to worship - and in all that time I did not dispute with anyone, neither did I stir up a crowd in the temple, the synagogues or in Jerusalem itself. They cannot prove any of the charges that they have brought against me.

ELDER 1   ELDER 2

(Mumbling and causing a disturbance)

FELIX

Silence ... let the accused proceed ...

PAUL

But this one thing is true ... I do worship the one who is called The Way .. and that according to them is a cult. But for me it is the worship of God according to all that was written in the law and the prophets concerning the Messiah. I have a firm hope in God ...

(Pointing to ELDERs)

... just as these men do ... that there will be a resurrection of the just and the unjust. My conscience is clear, I have not offended man or God.

ELDER 2

Nonsense! He was trying to profane the temple by bringing in Gentiles!

FELIX

Quiet everyone!

PAUL

Having been away for many years, I returned to Jerusalem to bring offerings to my nation .. and when I was in the temple, though I was not causing any trouble, the Jews brought accusations against me. And in fact, those who did, are not even here!

FELIX

(Addressing the ELDERS)

Is this true?

ELDER 1   ELDER 2

(General mumbling, FELIX takes down some notes)

PAUL

If they have accusations against me, they should be here. Otherwise, since these men ...

(Pointing to the ELDERs)

... know I stood before the council in Jerusalem, let them say what crimes I have committed. The one thing that I said ... and it is the same reason that I am before you today ... is that I believe in the resurrection of the dead! That and that alone is why I am here!

ELDER 1

Away with this fellow! He defies Moses!

FELIX

Enough! Enough! I have heard enough. Quiet now everyone! When Claudius Lysias, the garrison commander from Jerusalem, is come we will get to the bottom of this matter.

(To the GUARDS)

Take this man and keep him in custody.

(To PAUL)

Paul, you will be permitted to have visitors.

PAUL

(PAUL nods to FELIX and is taken away by the guards)

(BLACKOUT)

(END OF SCENE)

ACT 3
Scene 3

SETTING: A room in Caesarea - more than 2 years later.

AT RISE: FESTUS is sitting with some other men in the room. GUARD 4 and another guard are standing at the door.

NARRATOR

Felix left Paul bound for two years. Felix was recalled to Rome and replaced by Porcius Festus. When Paul was tried before Festus, he appealed to be judged in Rome before Augustus. As a Roman citizen this was his right. However, Festus had no crimes to lay against Paul so he asked King Agrippa, who was of Jewish background, to help him find a list of charges before sending Paul to Rome.

GUARD 4

Announcing the arrival of King Agrippa and Berenice!

(KING AGRIPPA and BERENICE come in with much fanfare)

FESTUS

Greetings good King Agrippa!

AGRIPPA

Greetings Festus. Long live Caesar! Greetings everyone.

(AGRIPPA and BERENICE sit next to FESTUS)

FESTUS

As I mentioned to you yesterday, for some reason, Felix left this man
called Paul in prison for the last two years. The chief priests and the
elders from Jerusalem could find no crime to lay against him.

AGRIPPA

Maybe this was one of those decisions that got Felix recalled to
Rome. There has been much unrest among the people.

FESTUS

Paul has appealed to Rome, however, I cannot deliver a man to die
without signifying the crimes to be brought against him. He keeps
talking about a man called Jesus who the Jews say is dead.

BERENICE

And what does Paul say?

FESTUS

That he is alive!

BERENICE

Oh goodness!

AGRIPPA

Yes, interesting. I would like to hear the man myself.

FESTUS

And you will, O King, ... perhaps with your knowledge of Jewish Law you can assist me in determining the nature of his crimes so that I have somewhat to write before sending him to Rome. It does not seem to me that he has done anything worthy of death.

AGRIPPA

Shall we hear what he has to say?

FESTUS

Guards! Bring the prisoner here!

GUARD 4

Yes sir.

(One guard leaves to get PAUL)

AGRIPPA

So he has appealed to Caesar, has he?

FESTUS

Yes, he is a Roman citizen .. free born apparently.

AGRIPPA

Then he has every right .. interesting fellow.

GUARD 4

(Appears at the door with PAUL who has chains around his feet and hands)

Paul the prisoner sir!

FESTUS

Yes, yes ... Paul come forward.

(PAUL stands before FESTUS and AGRIPPA)

FESTUS

(Making a speech)

King Agrippa and all you men who are present here today. You see this man whom all the Jews say should not live any longer. I have examined him and found nothing worthy of death. However, he himself has appealed to Augustus and I have decided to send him. Unfortunately, I have nothing to write against him. This is why I have brought Paul forth - especially before you O King Agrippa - that after we hear him together, I might have something to write for it did not seem reasonable to me to send a prisoner to Rome without specifying his crimes.

AGRIPPA

Paul, I permit you to answer for yourself.

(To the GUARD)

Unloose his hands.

(The GUARD takes the handcuffs off but leaves the chains on his feet)

PAUL

(Stretching forth his hand)

I am grateful that I have this opportunity to make my defense before you King Agrippa, especially because I know you are familiar with the customs of the Jews. I beg that you would patiently listen to me.

AGRIPPA

(Nods)

Proceed.

PAUL

The Judeans all know that in my early life I studied and spent much time in Jerusalem. I was an extremely strict Pharisee. And now here I am being judged simply for the promise that was made by God to my forefathers. This is the same promise that all the twelve tribes of Israel have been hoping for. And yet, they have accused me for the very same hope that they have!

Why should anyone think that it is unbelievable that God could raise the dead? At one time I was extremely hostile to Jesus the

Nazarene. I locked up many of the saints in prison because the chief priests had given me authority to do so ... and, what's more ... when they were put to death, I cast my vote against them!

AGRIPPA

Hmm.

BERENICE

Really? How dreadful!

PAUL

I even took them to the synagogue to punish them, to force them to blaspheme.

(Solemnly)

I was so furious with them, I started chasing them to foreign cities. And it was on one such trip, O king ...

(Pauses)

I was on the road to Damascus with letters from the chief priests to capture these rebels ... that I saw a light from heaven. It was so bright .. like the sun .. and it shone all around me. I fell to the ground and heard a voice, the voice of Jesus, asking me why I was persecuting him.

FESTUS

What?

PAUL

Yes, it was Jesus and he told me to get up. He said that he had
appeared to appoint me a servant and a witness of all that I had seen
and all that he would later show me. He said he was delivering me
from the people and sending me to the nations ... to open their eyes
so that they may turn from darkness to light, from the authority of
Satan to God and that they may receive forgiveness of sins and an
inheritance by believing in him.

(Turns directly towards AGRIPPA)

So, King Agrippa, I did not disobey his command but preached
Christ at Damascus, Jerusalem and throughout all the coasts of
Judea to both the Judeans and the Gentiles. I told them that they
must repent and turn to God and change their ways.

And because of this, the Jews caught me in the temple and wanted
to put me to death. But as always, God has helped me and with his
help I have continued witnessing to both small and great up until
this day. I've said nothing other than what Moses and the Prophets
said was going to happen - that the Messiah would suffer and then
be the first to rise from the dead and show light to the Judeans and
Gentiles.

FESTUS

Paul, you are clearly out of your mind! All your learning has made
you mad!

PAUL

I am not out of my mind most noble Festus but speak the truth!

(Pointing at AGRIPPA)

And the king knows all about these matters. I am confident that none of this has escaped his notice for these things were not done in a corner!

(To AGRIPPA)

King Agrippa ... do you believe, do you believe the prophets? Oh, I know that you believe.

AGRIPPA

(Unsure of what to say)

In such a short time like this, are you persuading me to become a Christian?

PAUL

I pray to God .. whether it takes a short time or a long time .. but that not only you but all those who hear me might become as I am ... that is, except for these chains.

BERENICE

(AGRIPPA, FESTUS, BERENICE, and others go to one side of the room. PAUL is left with the guard)

I do not think he has done anything wrong.

AGRIPPA

Surely nothing that is worthy of death.

BERENICE

And why should he be in prison? What is his crime?

FESTUS

That was precisely why I brought him before you .. to determine what I could write to the emperor. This has left me in rather a difficult predicament. All this talk of the Jewish Law and customs. Rome has no interest in that!

AGRIPPA

I do believe that this man could have been set free had he not appealed to Caesar.

(*They all turn and look at PAUL who is standing in chains*)

BERENICE

Seems rather a shame, brother, doesn't it?

AGRIPPA

Hmm.

(*BLACKOUT*)

(*END OF SCENE*)

ACT 3

Scene 4

SETTING: Two rooms side by side - one is a prison cell in
             Rome, the other a room far away in Ephesus.
             Several years later.

AT RISE: PAUL is sitting at a desk in the prison writing
             a letter. TIMOTHY is sitting at a desk in the
             other room reading a letter.

NARRATOR

Paul was sent to Rome and kept in custody for an initial period of
two years. After this it seems he was released for a period of time
and then incarcerated again under the emperor Nero. During his
time and imprisonments in Rome, Paul wrote several letters to the
churches. One of these was a letter to his beloved son in the faith,
Timothy.

TIMOTHY

(Reading)

Dear Timothy, God's blessings to you from God our Father and Christ Jesus our Lord. From the first time that we met I've always considered you as my son.

(Getting a little emotional)

Oh Master Paul ...

PAUL

(Writing)

I pray for you night and day and greatly desire to see you again. I remember the tears the last time we parted. You have always had such great faith - as did your grandmother, Lois, and your mother Eunice.

TIMOTHY

(Reading)

Just remember, God has not given us a spirit of fear but power, love and a sound mind. Don't ever be ashamed of your witness for Christ ... or of me who am now in prison.

(Stops reading)

I won't Paul, I will not be ashamed.

PAUL

(Writing)

Since you talk about Jesus Christ, you will definitely suffer for the gospel's sake.

(Stops writing and looks up talking to himself)

Of course, my son, you know this from all our journeys - the beatings, the ship wrecks, the false brethren, all the weariness, the prisons, swimming around a whole day and night in the sea, the robbers, hunger, thirst, cold ...

(Sighs. Starts writing again)

Because I am an apostle, I also suffer but I am not at all ashamed for I know whom I have believed. You must continue to teach what I have taught you. I'm sure that you've heard that all in Asia have deserted me.

TIMOTHY

(Reading)

Remember our friend Onesiphorus? He wasn't worried about being seen with me. Whenever he came to Rome he searched diligently and found me and visited me many times. May God be gracious and merciful to his household. Be strong in Christ Jesus Timothy and make sure you teach all that you know to faithful men. Don't get caught up in the affairs of everyday life - the gospel is always at stake.

PAUL

(Writing)

They think that I am a common criminal and as a result have bound me with these chains. But know this, the gospel can never be bound! Eternal life hangs in the balance.

TIMOTHY

(Knock at the door. TIMOTHY gets up and opens the door)

Hello Esther, Priscilla, Aquila! Greetings to you all!

ESTHER

(Carrying a blanket)

Greetings Timothy, we thought you might appreciate a visit. Are you busy?

TIMOTHY

Never too busy for all of you, do come in.

PRISCILLA

I brought some of my fresh bread.

ESTHER

And I brought you a new blanket that I just made.

TIMOTHY

Oh, you both are too kind … but I really appreciate it. Aquila, how is business?

AQUILA

Oh greetings Timothy. Business is as good as always, thanks be to God. Tents are in as high demand as in the days when Priscilla and I worked with Paul in Corinth. Oh, those were exciting times .. such a great response to the message of Christ.

TIMOTHY

Yes indeed .. yes …

(Getting a little pensive)

How times have changed …

ESTHER

What is wrong Timothy? You seem sad.

AQUILA

Are you in some sort of trouble?

TIMOTHY

Oh no, nothing like that. Just another letter from Rome.

AQUILA

Paul?

TIMOTHY

Yes dear friend, from Master Paul.

AQUILA

What did he write?

(TIMOTHY picks up the letter and reads part of it to them - silently)

PAUL

(Writing)

Make sure you study God's Word and keep in mind that the time is short. And be sure to teach it accurately. Do not get tricked into talking about foolish and ignorant controversies ... that is just a waste of your time.

ESTHER

That is good advice Timothy ... Onesiphorus told me that Paul had encouraged him in much the same way when he visited him in Rome. But I suspect there is more than that ...

TIMOTHY

(Reading silently again)

PAUL

(Writing)

I must tell you that times of great difficulty are ahead. Men and their passions will be fueled into much evil. They will fiercely resist

the truth that you speak. But you know how I have lived, my son ..
with patience, faith and love. Remember the persecution we faced
at Antioch, Iconium and Lystra?

TIMOTHY

Those were difficult times.

PAUL

(Writing)

But what happened? God delivered us out of them all! And if you are
going to serve him, you will suffer persecution. Even though times
will be difficult, you make sure you stick to the Scriptures that you
have known from a child. They have taught you of salvation .. they
have pointed the way to Jesus Christ and it is the Scriptures that will
make sure you are ready for anything that comes your way.

PRISCILLA

It was the Scriptures that turned the entire city of Corinth around
and provided such great deliverance. And then again at Ephesus ...
and everywhere it was spoken. And yes, there was always persecution
but God was greater. Is there more Timothy?

TIMOTHY

(Reading)

He said to make sure that, whether it's convenient or not, I preach
the Word. The times are coming when people will not listen to the
truth .. they shall turn their ears away and believe myths ...

(Getting choked up)

... and then ... and then ...

AQUILA

What is it dear boy?

PAUL

(Writing)

I am now ready to be offered and the time of my departure is at hand.

(Pauses. Starts writing again)

I have fought a good fight. I have finished the race. I have kept the faith. When the Lord appears to gather the church, he will reward what I have done ... and not just me, but all those who look eagerly to his appearing.

Timothy, do your best to come visit me as soon as you can.

PRISCILLA

Goodness Timothy, are you going to go?

TIMOTHY

I will do my best if I can make it before the winter.

PAUL

(Writing)

Many who were close to me have forsaken me. Luke is still with me. At my first defense there was no one with me ... I pray that it will not be charged against them. But the Lord was always with me and gave me strength so that I could continue to preach. And he will always deliver. Glory to him forever and ever.

(GUARD 5 appears at the door of the cell. PAUL rolls up the letter and walks over to him)

GUARD 5

How are you Master Paul? Many of my friends in the Praetorian guard wish to hear you again.

PAUL

Hmm .. it would be my privilege time and circumstances allowing. In the mean time, can you do something for me?

GUARD 5

Yes of course .. whatever I can.

PAUL

Can you make sure that Luke gets this letter? It is to be sent to Timothy with haste.

GUARD 5

Yes Master Paul .. right away.

(Hastens off with the letter. PAUL sits at the table and bows his head in prayer)

TIMOTHY

(Indicating PRISCILLA and AQUILA)

Then he sends greetings to the both of you …

AQUILA

May God's blessings be upon him at this time and always.

PRISCILLA

As always .. thinking of everyone else but himself.

TIMOTHY

And to you Esther ... he sends greetings to the household of
Onesiphorus.

ESTHER

God bless him .. but .. but .. what is all this about his departure ..
what he said about finishing the race?

(Everyone is silent)

PAUL

(GUARD 6 appears at the door of the cell and bangs on the bars. PAUL
looks up)

GUARD 6

It is time.

PAUL

Come quickly Lord Jesus, come quickly.

(GUARD 6 opens the door and leads PAUL away. Everyone stands in
silence for a moment)

TIMOTHY

(To the audience)

And how about you gentle man or gentle lady? In your journey in this life, have you had the blessing of being introduced to the babe from Bethlehem? Is it truth that you seek or are you more fond of myths? Well, if it is indeed the truth that you desire, might we be so bold as to suggest making Jesus your Lord and believing with all your heart that God has raised him from the dead? But I must warn you .. if our brief time together in the presence of the Apostle Paul has given you any indication of what lies ahead .. there is no guarantee of a trouble free life. The Scriptures themselves in fact say the exact opposite, as our beloved Paul wrote, those who desire to live a godly life in Christ Jesus will be persecuted. The road is not for the faint of heart or the weak of soul … not at all. But wait, there is hope after all! If you are faint of heart and weak of soul, do not be alarmed. Christ himself shall give you the strength and courage you need. All you need do is to call upon the name of Jesus Christ and you will not be disappointed. But why, you might ask, make a decision that leads to sure persecution? Well that is simple, it is the only road to eternal life and an incorruptible inheritance reserved in heaven for you.

So, fellow traveler … do you dare to run the race with us?

(BLACKOUT)

(END OF ACT 3)

SET AND STAGE SUGGESTIONS

Though this play has 3 acts and many scenes, the set design can be done in a very minimal manner. The following are some suggestions regarding the <u>basics</u> required for each scene with emphasis on key scene elements. Obviously, any prop additions can be made for greater effect as deemed suitable.

Act 1

Scene 1 : A Judean Courtroom

- Chairs in a semi-circle for the council members

Scene 2 : Outside the City

- An open area
- Piles of rocks (not real!) around the area (for the stoning)
- Blood effects due to the stoning

Scene 3 : Room in a House

- Chairs for several people in a semi-circle around the teacher (Josiah)
- A door at the back of the room (where Paul and the soldiers will enter)

Scene 4 : On the Road to Damascus

- An open road
- Some shrubs or bushes on the side
- A bright blinding light from above (when Jesus speaks) – the light might be accompanied by a swooshing sound to startle the men

Scene 5 : Two Rooms in Two Separate Houses (side by side)

- Stage split down the middle with divider
- Left side – House 1/Room 1 – a single chair (for Paul). A door at the back of the room – this is where Ananias will enter
- Right side – House 2/Room 2 – a bench (Ananias kneeling beside it praying)
- When Jesus speaks to Ananias, it will be quite effective if Paul looks in the direction of Room 2 as if he can see what is going on (the Bible says that Paul saw a vision of a man named Ananias coming to him). If Paul looks in that direction when Jesus is speaking, it should provide the effect of him seeing a vision

Act 2

Scene 1 : A Market in Lystra

- A road on left of stage leading to a market on the right
- A few tables with food, etc. for the market
- Some piles of rocks around the market (for the stoning)
- Blood effects for the stoning

Scene 2 : Outside city of Troas

- Open area with a fire pit
- When man of Macedonia speaks in a vision, it might be effective to have a misty appearance above the fire pit

Scene 3 : City of Philippi – House of Lydia and Outside

- A divider wall to the right side of stage with door into house. A couple of chairs inside the house
- Left side of stage – a street outside the house – some props to indicate a street (lamp post, shrub, etc.)
- Blood effects for the beating

Scene 4 : A Prison in Philippi

- A prison room with rats, a prison door on the right side of the cell
- Stocks for Paul and Silas or simply chains
- A single candle in the prison

Act 3

Scene 1 : House of Philip

- A table with several chairs
- A door to the right of the room (door leads to offstage kitchen)
- A door at the back of the room (where Agabus will enter)

Scene 2 : A Roman Court in Caesarea

- Chairs arranged in a court room setting
- Main chair for Felix

Scene 3 : A Room in Caesarea

- Main chairs for Festus, Agrippa and Berenice
- Other chairs for spectators
- Door to the right (where Paul will enter)

Scene 4 : Two Rooms (side by side)

- Stage divided in center with divider
- Left Room – a house in Ephesus. A desk and four chairs. A door at the back of the room (where Esther, Priscilla and Aquila will enter)
- Right Room – a prison cell in Rome. Single chair with primitive desk with a single candle. There is a door to the right of the cell
- It will be very important in this scene to get the timing synchronized between Paul speaking and Timothy speaking. Since Timothy is later reading what Paul is actually writing in the scene, it will be a wonderful effect if the back and forth is timed very well. Stage lighting (slightly dimming one side or the other when the speakers switch might also be helpful if not too distracting)

The words spoken by Jesus Christ are taken from the English Standard Version (2016), Acts, Chapter 9:4-16 and Acts 26: 15-18.

ABOUT THE AUTHOR

Raj Hans holds a Bachelor of Engineering from McGill University and a Bachelor of Theology and has been involved in Biblical research for many years. His passion is to help people to understand the Bible for themselves. He is involved in Christian ministry in a home church setting along with producing content for his bibleharbor. com website. His play "Running the Race" represents the synthesis of much research involving the Apostle Paul. He can be reached at r.hans@wordharbor.com

Printed in the United States
by Baker & Taylor Publisher Services

Printed in the United States
by Baker & Taylor Publisher Services